Piano Theory W

Book 2

Authors
**Barbara Kreader, Fred Kern,
Phillip Keveren, Mona Rejino,
Karen Harrington**

*Director,
Educational Keyboard Publications*
Margaret Otwell

Editor
Carol Klose

Illustrator
Fred Bell

FOREWORD

The **Piano Theory Workbooks** present theory writing assignments that coordinate page-by-page with the **Piano Lessons** books in the **Hal Leonard Student Piano Library**.

Spike, Party Cat and friends guide the student through fun and creative activities that introduce the language of music and its symbols for sound, silence and rhythm. Ear training exercises and basic theory help students learn to write and play the music they are learning as well as the music they create themselves.

Best wishes,

Barbara Kreader   Fred Kern   Phillip Keveren

Mona Rejino   Karen Harrington

ISBN 0-7935-7688-1

CORPORATION
7777 W. BLUEMOUND RD. P.O. BOX 13819 MILWAUKEE, WI 53213

Visit Hal Leonard Online at
www.halleonard.com

The Grand Staff – A Musical Map

Help Inspector Hound complete his map.

1. Write the names of the blank keys on the keyboard.
2. Trace the missing notes on the staff.
3. Color the following keys on the keyboard and notes on the staff:

Red for C   **Blue for D**   **Green for E**

Write the note names in the blanks below.
Your teacher will play one measure from each blue box. Circle the example you hear.

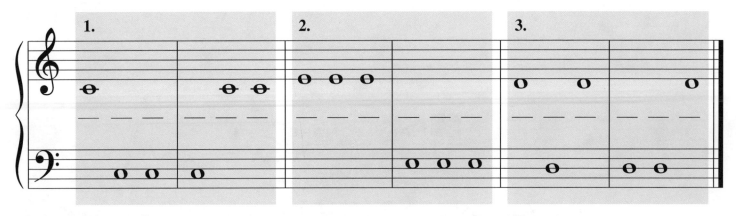

Drawing Notes on the Staff

Practice drawing stems.

Notes on the third line and higher have stems on the left going down.

Notes on the second space and lower have stems on the right going up.

Add a stem to each note.

Add a stem to each note.

Spike is conducting *Ode To Joy*. Help him write the cello part. It is written in the bass clef and uses the same notes as the melody in the violin part. Draw the missing notes in the blue boxes.

violin

cello

Violin

Cello

Play the two parts hands separately, then hands together.

3

Rests

When Pig and Goat tried to play *Old MacDonald Had A Farm*,
they had trouble because the rests were missing!

Trace and fill in each rest and draw three more.

Quarter Rest   **Half Rest**   **Whole Rest**

Help Pig and Goat complete each measure by drawing the correct rest in each blue box.

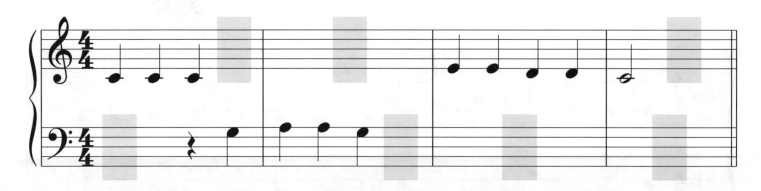

Playing on C D E F G

Party Cat is trying to trick you by playing one wrong note in each song below.
Play each song. As your teacher plays Party Cat's version of each one,
circle the one note he plays wrong.

Teacher's Examples on pg. 40

Use with Lesson Book 2, pg. 7

Rhythm Detective

Find the missing measures!

Each rhythm in Column A is missing its second measure.
You will find it in Column B.

Your teacher will clap each two-measure pattern.
Connect the first measure in Column A to the correct
second measure in Column B.

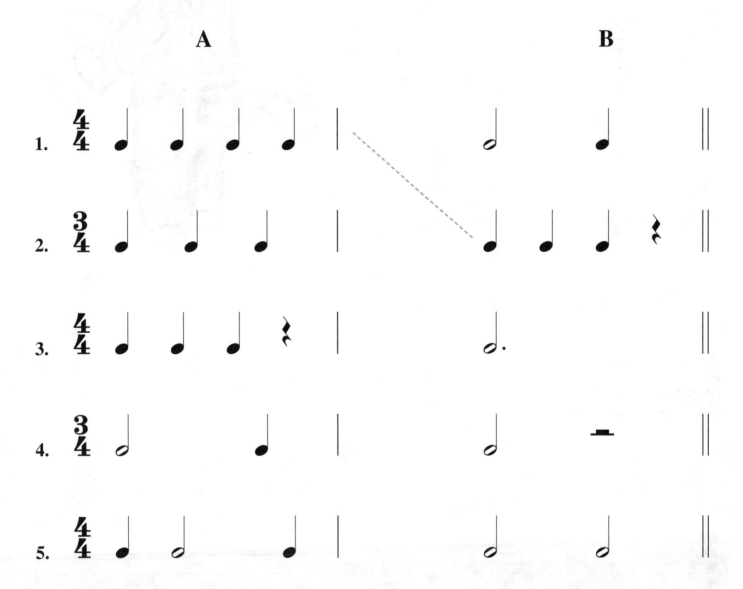

Note Name Review

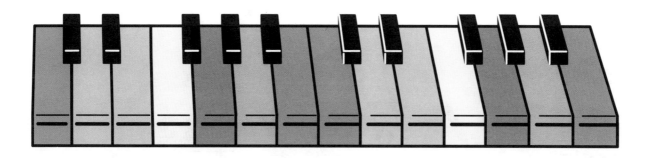

Complete this picture using the colors in the keyboard guide.

Use with Lesson Book 2, pg. 9

Harmonic or Melodic?

Each of Party Cat's balloons has either a melodic or harmonic interval.
Circle the correct answer.

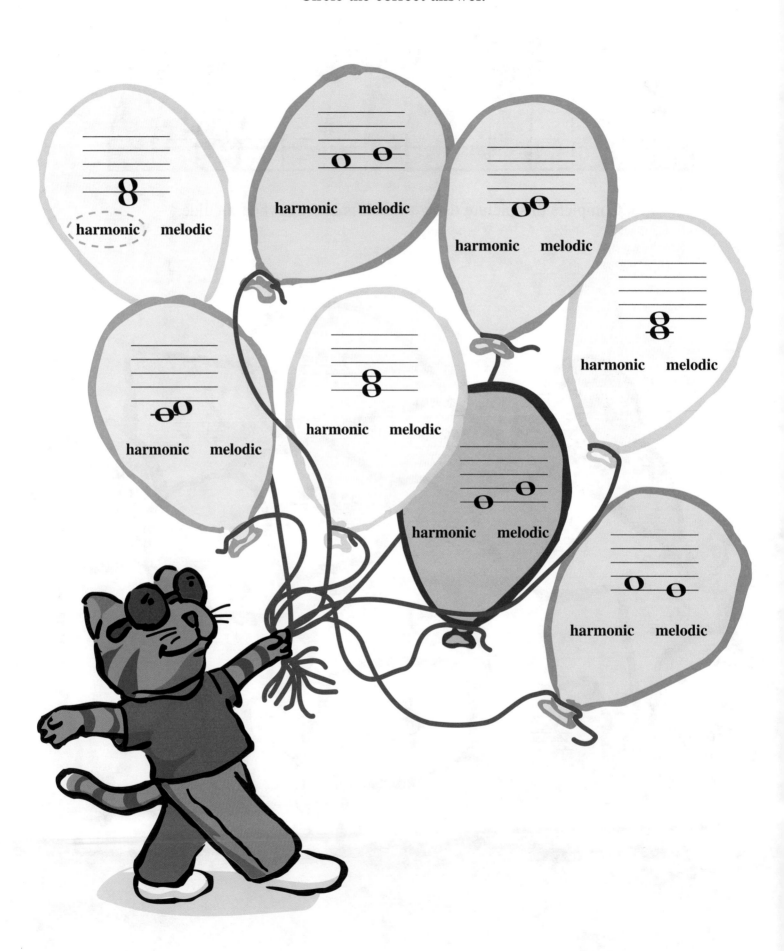

Harmonic 2nds and 3rds

In each of Spike's balloons, draw a whole note that is a
harmonic 2nd or 3rd above each given note.

Use with Lesson Book 2, pg. 10

Legato or Staccato?

Your teacher will play six musical examples.
Circle *Legato* if the music sounds smooth and connected.
Circle *Staccato* if the music sounds short and separated.

1.	
Legato	**Staccato**

2.	
Legato	**Staccato**

3.	
Legato	**Staccato**

4.	
Legato	**Staccato**

5.	
Legato	**Staccato**

6.	
Legato	**Staccato**

Drawing Legato and Staccato Marks

Bear has composed some music.
Help him add the legato marks (slurs)
or staccato marks to each example.

1. Add slurs to each phrase, then play this song.
2. Circle the best song title.

Skating

Popping Corn

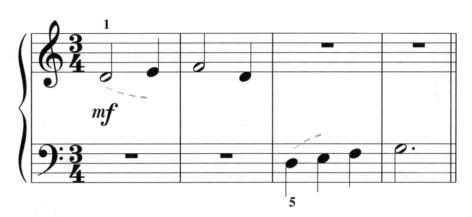

1. Add a staccato mark to each note, then play this song.
2. Circle the best song title.

Jumping Jacks

Sliding

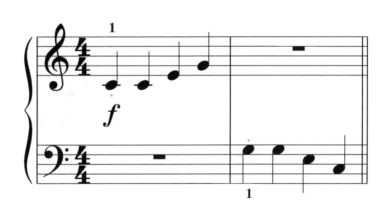

Match the mood of these titles by adding either slurs or staccato marks to the music.

Sneaking on Tiptoe   Smooth as Silk

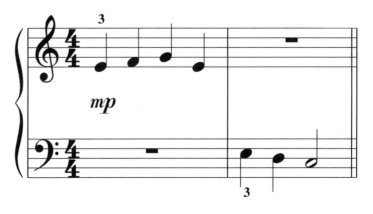

11

4ths

Match each 4th on the staff to the same 4th on the keyboard
by drawing a line from Column A to Column B.

A
                                                  B

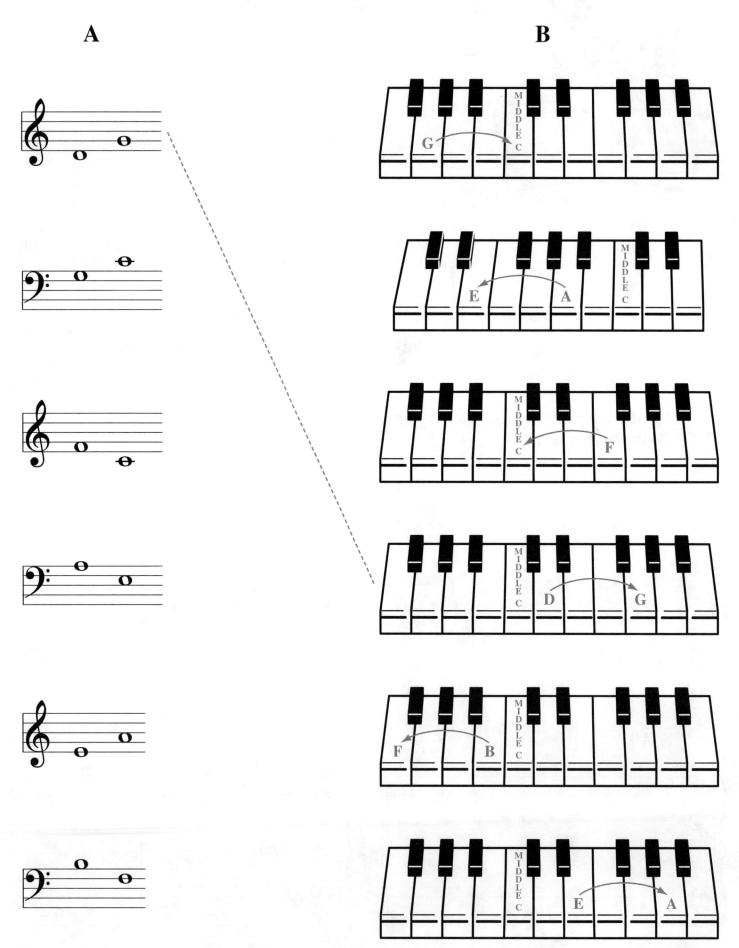

Intervalasaurus

Complete this picture by drawing a straight line from one note to the next.
Write the name of the intervals in the blue boxes.

13

Upbeat Melodies

Party Cat needs to sharpen his rhythmic skills before his next jam session.

1. Write the correct time signature in each blue box.
2. Write the counts in the blanks.
3. Play each melody.

1.

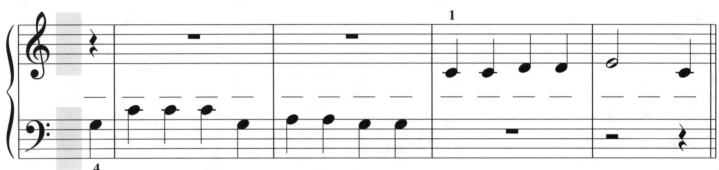

2.

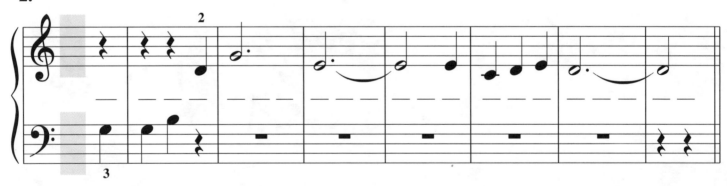

3.

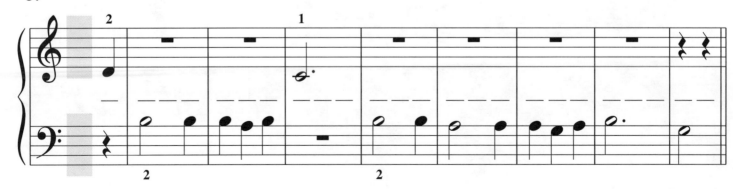

Measuring Upbeats

Duck is playing the drums for an upcoming dance at Spike's house.
Help him add the bar lines to his music. Every example has an upbeat.

1. Trace the barline that separates the upbeat from the first full measure. Then add bar lines to complete each example. Because of the upbeat, the last measure will be incomplete.
2. Clap and count each pattern.

15

Dynamic Detective

Add your own dynamic marks to the music below.

1. Play each piece below.

2. Choose either *p*, *f* or *ff* and draw the symbol
   in the ▨ boxes in measures 1 and 4.

3. Choose either ⬐═══◁ or ▷═══⬎ and draw the symbol in the
   ▨ box in measure 3.

Painted Rocking Horse

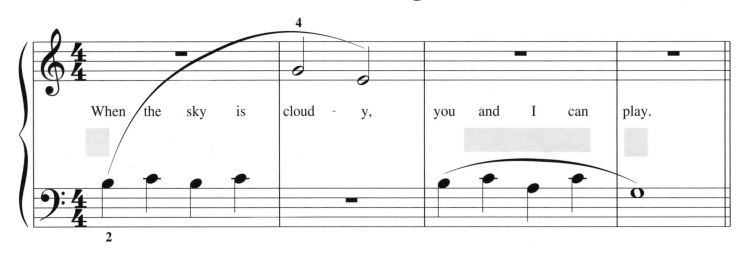

Hoedown

W Rong Rhythms

Sometimes Party Cat forgets to wind the Jazz Clock and its rhythmic ticking gets mixed up.

Each measure below should have four counts.
Put an "X" through any of the measures that have the wrong number of counts.

1.

2.

3.

4.

5.

6.

17

Use with Lesson Book 2, pg. 20

Beeline to the Intervals

1. Draw a line from each bee to a flower that matches it.
2. Color the flowers using this guide:

2nds Orange	3rds Blue	4ths Yellow	5ths Red

Ties or Slurs?

Study each example.
Are the notes connected by a tie or a slur?
Circle the correct answer.

A **tie** is a curved line that connects notes of the **same** pitch.

A **slur** is a curved line that connects notes of **different** pitch.

tie   slur

tie   slur

tie   slur

tie   slur

tie   slur

tie   slur

tie   slur

tie   slur

tie   slur

Use with Lesson Book 2, pg. 23

Interval Bounce

Measure the distance of each basketball bounce.

1. Put a "1" in each blue ball and continue counting every space and line to the next brown basketball. Write the name of each interval in the box below each basketball.

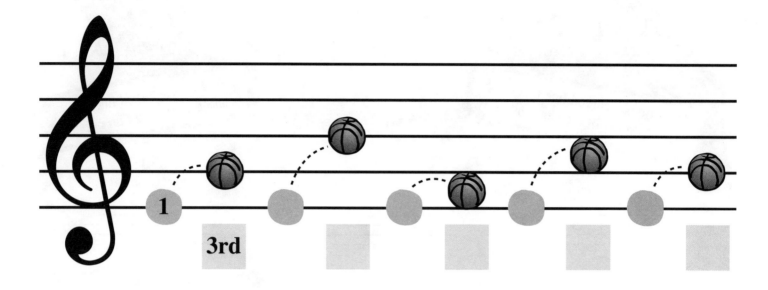

2. Put a "1" in each blue ball. Draw a basketball on the line or space that matches the name of the interval.

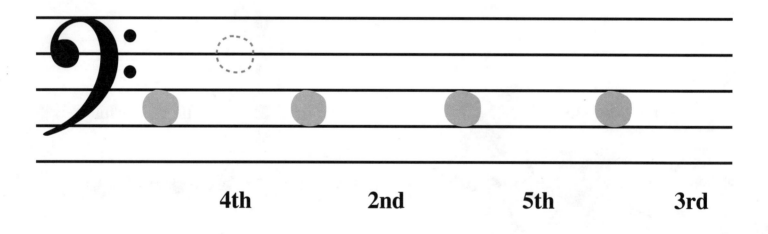

4th   **2nd**   **5th**   **3rd**

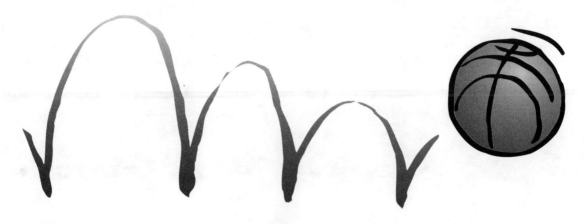

It's a Tie!

Some rhythms sound the same but <u>look</u> different.
Match the measures that sound alike by drawing a line
from Column A to Column B.

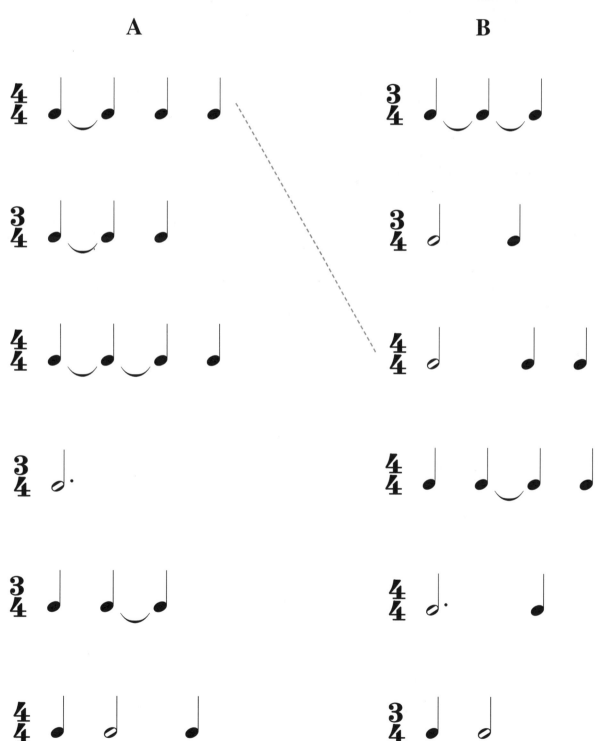

Sharps

SHARP

♯

Play the next key to the right, either black or white.

1. Trace the sharps below.

space sharp   **line sharp**

2. Draw a sharp sign in the box before each note.
3. Write the name of each note in the blank below it.

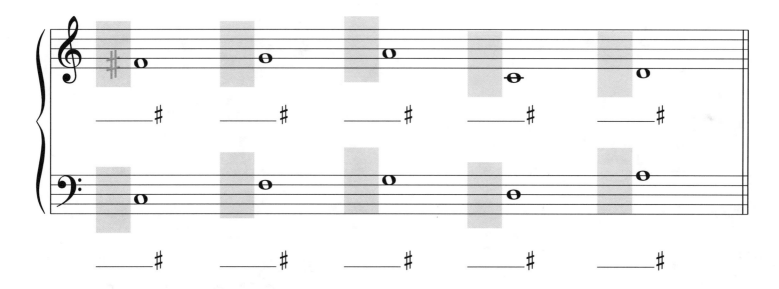

_____ ♯   _____ ♯   _____ ♯   _____ ♯   _____ ♯

_____ ♯   _____ ♯   _____ ♯   _____ ♯   _____ ♯

4. Write the name of the sharp key in the blank above each key.

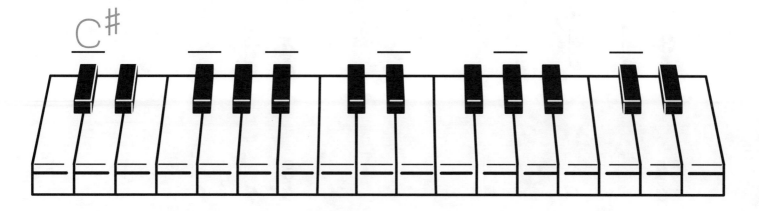

Listening to Form –
Is it A or B?

Bear will show you how sections
of music fit together by using his **A** and **B** balloons.

The **A Section** is the
main theme of the piece.

The **B Section** is a
different but related theme.

Color this **A** balloon red.

Color this **B** balloon blue.

1. As you listen to your teacher play each piece, identify the **A** and **B** sections.
2. As you listen a second time, your teacher will play only the **A Section** or only the **B Section** of each piece. Color the balloons that match the sections you hear.

Twinkle Twinkle Little Star

Pierrot

Old MacDonald Had A Farm

Teacher's Examples on pg. 40

Use with Lesson Book 2, pg. 30

Flats

FLAT

♭

Play the next key to the left, either black or white.

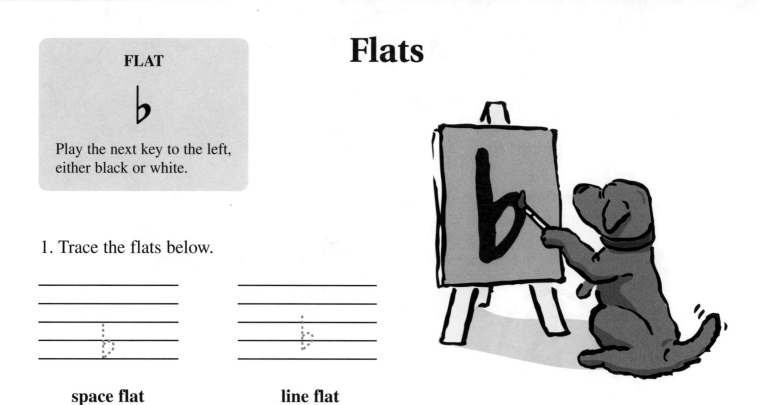

1. Trace the flats below.

space flat   **line flat**

2. Draw a flat sign in the box before each note.
3. Write the name of each note in the blank below it.

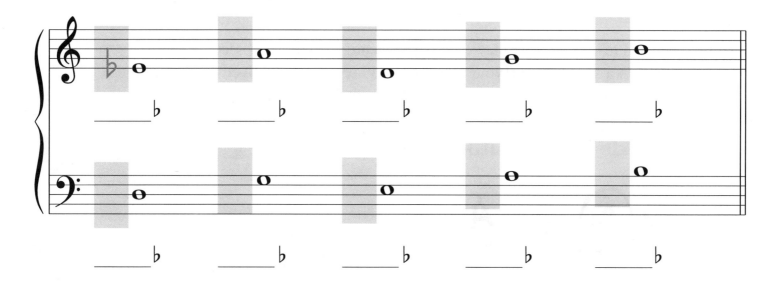

_____ ♭   _____ ♭   _____ ♭   _____ ♭   _____ ♭

_____ ♭   _____ ♭   _____ ♭   _____ ♭   _____ ♭

4. Write the name of the flat key in the blank above each key.

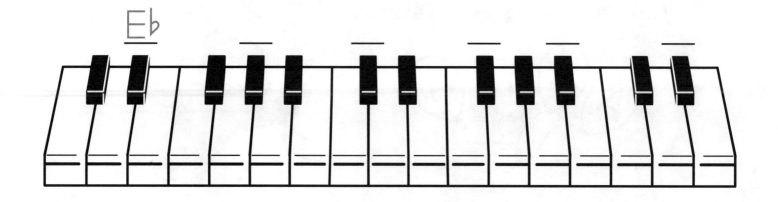

E♭

Ritard (*rit.*)

Circle the things that are slowing down little by little.

1. Play and sing the song below keeping a steady tempo.
2. Write a *rit.* sign in the blue box.
3. Play and sing the song again, gradually slowing the tempo in the last two measures.

Falling Asleep

25

Use with Lesson Book 2, pg. 34

Naturals

Trace the naturals below.

space natural   **line natural**

Draw a natural sign in the box before each note
and write the name of each note in the blank below it.

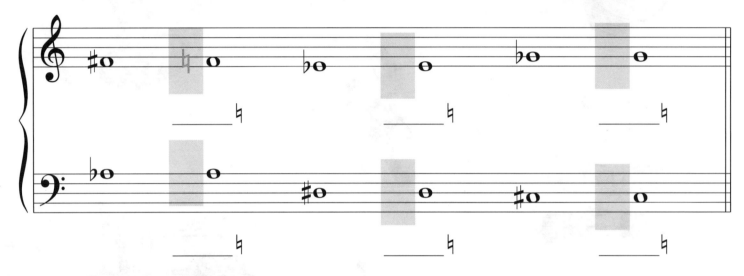

A sharp or flat lasts for one measure, unless a natural sign cancels it.
Write the correct answers below.

1. How many notes are played
as **F♯** in each measure?

2. How many notes are played
as **E♭** in each measure?

3. How many notes are played
as **B♭** in each measure?

4. How many notes are played
as **C♯** in each measure?

Sign Quest

1. Write a sharp (♯) sign in front of all the **F's**.
2. Write a flat (♭) sign in front of all the **E's**.
3. Play the song and give it a title.

Title: _____

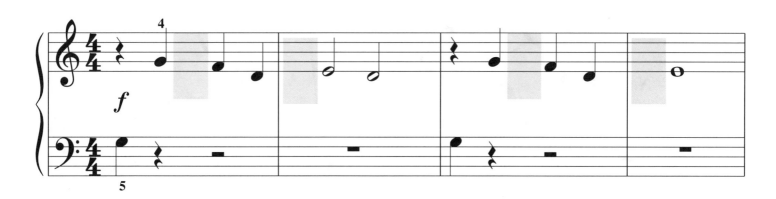

Use with Lesson Book 2, pg. 36

Symbol Road

Symbol Sam the Signpost Man is painting all the signs along Symbol Road.
Complete the job by drawing the correct musical symbol for each signpost.

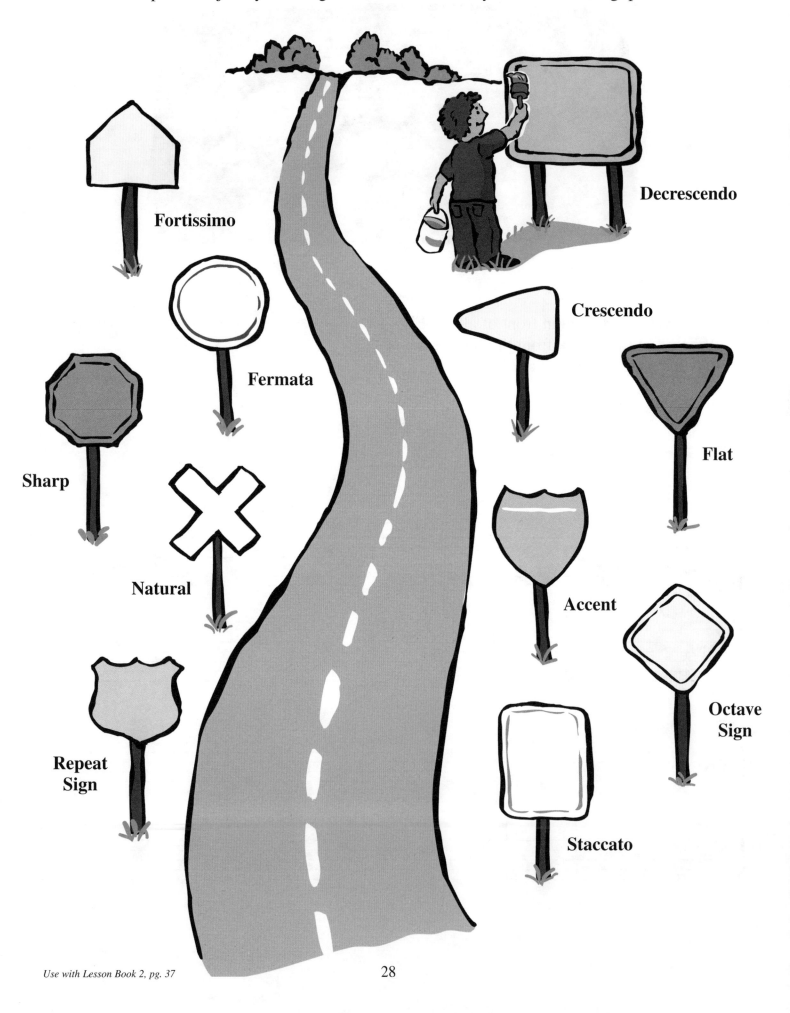

Fortissimo

Decrescendo

Fermata

Crescendo

Sharp

Flat

Natural

Accent

Octave Sign

Repeat Sign

Staccato

The Grand Staff – Playing on B C D

1. Write the names of the blank keys on the keyboard.
2. Trace the missing notes on the staff and draw a line to the correct key on the keyboard.

Complete the mystery tune below by drawing the missing quarter notes in the blue boxes. Play the piece and write its title.

Title: _____

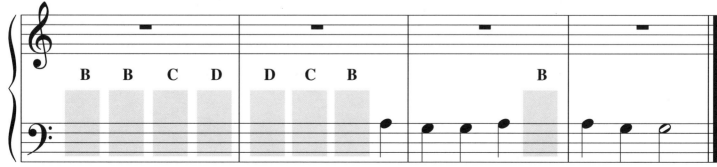

Ledger Lines

Party Cat is studying for a theory test.
Help him learn what ledger lines are by completing the sentence below.

1. Draw a ledger line D note in each blue box below.
2. Write the note names in the blanks below each note.

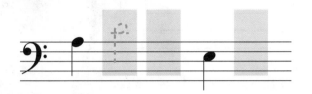

Lines   __   __   __   __   __

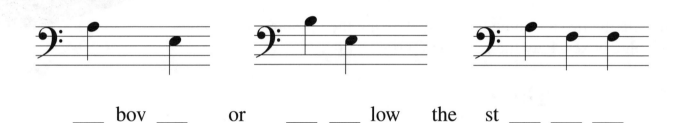

__ bov __   or   __ __ low   the   st __ __ __

are   __ __ lle __

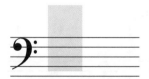

le __ ger   lines.

Spike is Puzzled!

Spike loves crossword puzzles.
Help him complete each word by writing the note names in the blanks.

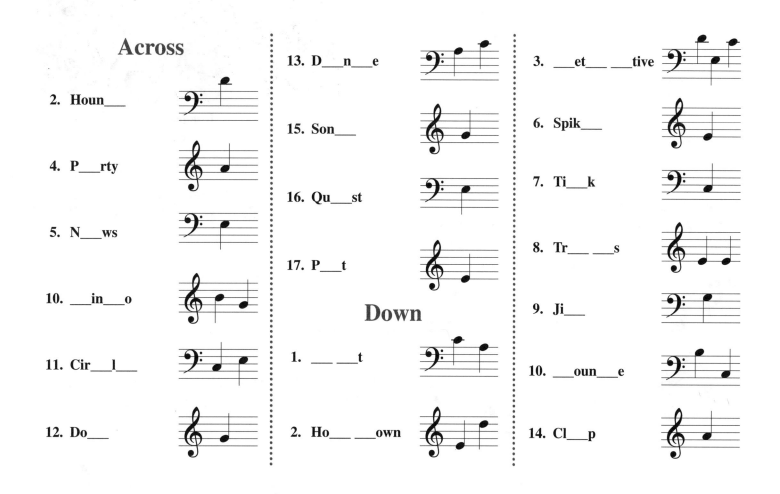

Across

2. Houn___

4. P___rty

5. N___ws

10. ___in___o

11. Cir___l___

12. Do___

13. D___n___e

15. Son___

16. Qu___st

17. P___t

Down

1. ___ ___t

2. Ho___ ___own

3. ___et___ ___tive

6. Spik___

7. Ti___k

8. Tr___ ___s

9. Ji___

10. ___oun___e

14. Cl___p

31

Use with Lesson Book 2, pg. 42

Octave Sign *8va--*

Bear, Party Cat and Spike play in the band.

1. Play *Pop Goes The Weasel* and decide which instrument would play the high, the middle, and the low parts.
2. Write the name of the correct instruments in each blue box.

flute   trumpet   tuba

Use with Lesson Book 2, pg. 43

G A B C D Mysteries

1. Party Cat went shopping and lost his sunglasses.
   Complete the story below to find out what happened.

Party Cat left his sunglasses in a _____ when he was

riding in a _____ . We hope his _____

won't be mad at that _____ cat!

2. Bear has lost his music assignment. Where is it?

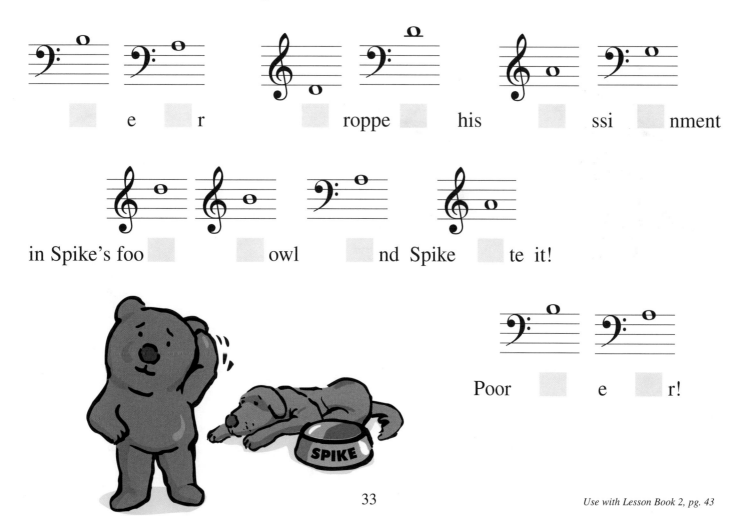

___ e ___ r ___ roppe ___ his ___ ssi ___ nment

in Spike's foo ___ ___ owl ___ nd Spike ___ te it!

Poor ___ e ___ r!

33

Use with Lesson Book 2, pg. 43

Dynamic Play

Party Cat is sneaking up on Spike.
Guide his footsteps by writing the dynamic marks
from softest to loudest in the boxes below.

Add music to this story by playing the notes next to each dynamic marking.

Upbeat

Help the leprechaun feel the upbeats.

1. Every example has two upbeats. First, trace the barline that separates the upbeats, then add barlines to complete each example. Because of the upbeat, the last measure will be incomplete.

2. Write the counts in the blanks and clap each example.

35

Use with Lesson Book 2, pg. 45

Rhythm Detective

Find the missing notes and rests!

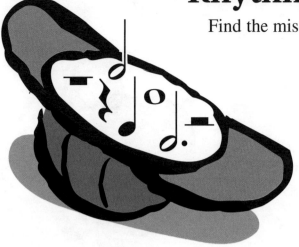

1. Draw the missing note or rest in the blue boxes.
   Use each symbol from the detective's hat only once.
2. Clap and count each example.

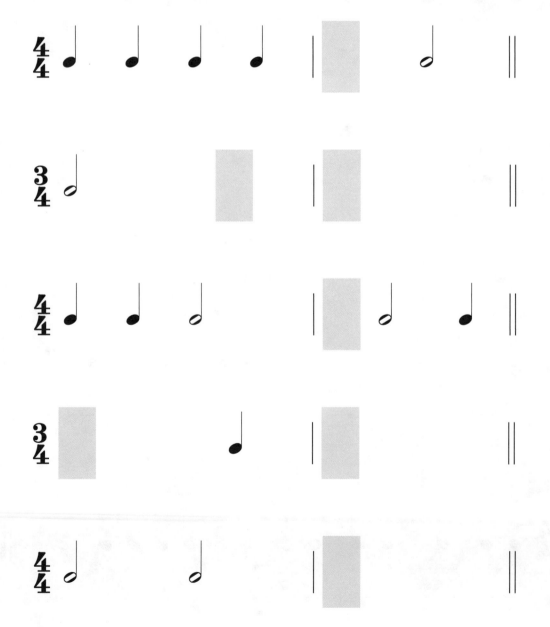

Interval Food

It's dinnertime and Spike is hungry.
Find out what he likes to eat.

Go to the keyboard and play each clue.
Write the name of the last key you land
on in the blue box.

1. Start on C   3rd ↘   2nd ↗   2nd ↗

2. Start on F   2nd ↘   3rd ↗   2nd ↗

3. Start on D   3rd ↗   2nd ↘   4th ↘

4. Start on A   5th ↗   3rd ↘   2nd ↘

5. Start on F   4th ↘   3rd ↗   4th ↗

6. Start on B   5th ↗   5th ↗   4th ↘

7. Start on C   3rd ↘   2nd ↗   4th ↗

Use with Lesson Book 2, pg. 46

Interval Roundup

1. Using the arrows as your guide, draw whole notes to build the intervals on each staff.
2. Draw X's on the keys that match each interval.

Relay Review

Spike and Party Cat are racing to finish their theory workbook.
Match the correct answers by drawing a line from Column A to Column B.
Record your time in the box at the end of each race.

START

A	B
	Bass C D E
	tie
	staccato
	fermata
	legato
	harmonic 2nd
	harmonic 3rd
	upbeat
	harmonic 4th
	melodic 4th
	accent

START

A	B
pp	slow tempo gradually
rit.	melodic 5th
	octave sign
	crescendo
	flat
	slur
	ledger line D
8va - - - ⌐	pianissimo
♭	decrescendo
	sharp
	harmonic 5th

The winner is:

_____

FINISH Seconds

FINISH Seconds

39

Use with Lesson Book 2, pg. 48

Teacher's Examples

Page 2 (Play)

Page 5 (Play)   * = Party Cat's wrong note.

Page 6 (Clap)

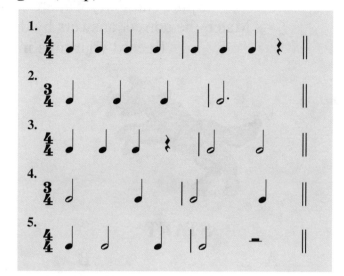

Page 10 (Play)

Page 23 (Play)   1. Play all.
                      2. Play only the section indicated.

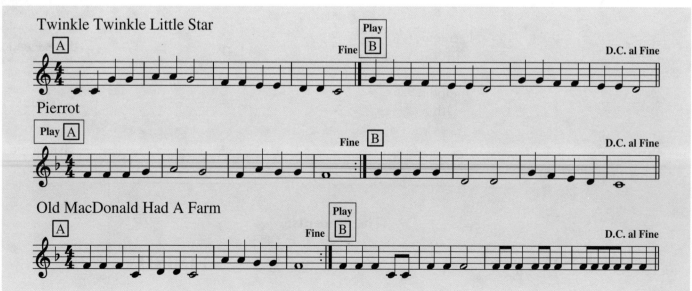